One Free
Crystal Moment

Poems by
ELIZABETH SHAW

Edited by Rebecca Salome

Whitewing Press
TUCSON

First printing 2011

Whitewing Press
Box 65539
Tucson, Arizona 85728-5539

ISBN 978-1-888965-10-0
Library of Congress Control Number 2010941422

Contents

Collected Poems

Review

There was one splash of scarlet
and much that was gray peace
and much that was kneeling
at an altar in tear-clad repentance,
and one free crystal moment—that was love.

[1939]

Of Marriage

There is a symmetry of thinking
and a syncopation of action,
a recurrent freshening
of the showers of living,
and a well-justified glow
around the dawn of the future.

[DECEMBER 1943]

Flight

This dreaming into death upon a wing
is music to us listening ones below
among whom certain wise hearts know
that dreaming and not dying is the thing
that conquers. This glorious chariot of beauty
though ironclad headed for destruction,
when fiery whip lash out and fling it all to nothing.

It is said the flying ones are kings
more rightly then the rulers of the past,
firm-rooted in the earth wherein they sleep,
whose tiresome journeys ended all at last
in war or bed of glory and long sorrowing.
Now where heroes fall, a wisp of smoke to fly
and silver veil is pulled across the sky.

[1943]

Washington Beside the Potomac

Resting upon the bosom of earth,
beside the smiling River, you can hear
the squall of a new world emerging from
the womb of history. This is Washington,
known far and wide as the City of Freedom.

They say the sun trembles before the City,
outdone by the whiteness of its marble.
To strike its powerful balance, the sun
frowns alike on white dome and crumbling walls.
Of both there is abundance.

The City is proud. Like a white peacock
it spreads and swings its fan beside the River,
like a princess it moves beneath the blossoms
in a dance of classic grace
before the high altar of its fathers.

Before the whole world the City stands,
a youth in white armor, gazing far
beyond the River, singing songs of strength
and raising a shield of bright promise
to other cities across the sea.

Still across the City lies the shadow
of another youth, far-seeing, strong
but without a shield. He is neither like the marble
nor the sun. And the City owns him not.
He has no armor and no songs of a new world.

For him there is hot earth and the River
where pollution runs. For him the singing youth
is master, the armor a shining deception,
and the brightness on the shield
a blinding lie.

[JUNE 1943]

Who and What Are We?

You are a city, resounding, great,
I am a small and hidden street
where trees bend to grace the children's game,
where tiny shops stay open late,
and hawkers forever call your name.

You are a mountain looming tall,
I am a dislodged stone,
tumbling, rolling there and here
where I land at the feet of my own.
You are a giant breaker,
I am a drifting shore.
I curve and I invite,
you thunder and you smite,
I await your coming more.
You are an eagle, gold, aloft,
I, a feather from your breast.
A random breeze has carried me
up, upward to your own Aerie
where, if you please, I rest.

You are sound at the moment when
it strikes the air to ride the wind.
I, an echo, resound, repeat
you, again, again.

[1961]

The Weaver's Song

Row by row
click and throw,
See life in its mystery grow

Weave into its grayer folds
italic of impassioned thought.
Knit emphasis in every word,
twist intricately the strands,
pull them together, taut as truth.
Their ordered joining holds.

Wind into the cloth of gold
the dark, dark thread of pain
for contrast and reminder.
Thread it through the fabric bold.
As for fading and forgetting,
pain will find a way.

Cover conscience with bright thread.
Breathe fire into its forms.
In every inch where spirit glows,
as swift as shuttle warps ahead,
newfound joys bloom into sight.
Love may turn the mantle red.

[1965]

The Music

Sweet round space of bird sound
like a drop of water
falling musically to itself,
carrying the tune for love.
Sweet transparent windfingers
caressing upon caressing,
coaxing and enjoining though
the night has scarcely room enough,
so numerous are the kissings.

Sweet dark sounds of wordless voices,
low notes with rhythmed sighing
as we are swaying to, and over us
are branches swaying fro.

Sweet endlessness of stretching
arms around, lip to brow,
cool sole placed on cool thigh,
warm cheek against broad back
or laid on breast, where heartbeat is.

From the newly swelling sea of love
passion comes up as a wave
falls rushing from its foaming head,
engulfing us until the stars pale.

[1966]

Non-Stop to the East

Adrift in a white world
confused by whirling vision,
reassured by ground's abstraction,
and linear everydayness
we think we understand
seeing mountains not as barriers
but past dynamics of a land
asleep in winter light
and by translucence showing
peaks subject to the rule of space,
as we are captive of the miles beneath.

Wind goes past us like a puff of ice
dissolving in a curtain of grey mist,
and we think it may have rained
until we fly around that curtain,
see it glistening with sun,
burning away the snowfields
from a geometric world
that bends beneath our wing—offering, tilted and
planed,
an ocean to our unbelieving eyes.

[1966]

The Parting of Gods and Men

From our near and village world
the gods of the years have gone away,
have left our hearth where evermore
they stoked the fires to warm our sleep,
have left our board where they had blessed
the findings of our hunt and fields,
have left the bedside vigil kept
to hail the bursting of the maiden bud
and guard new entrants from the dark
whose secrets they have under stood.

When they moved up to the small hill
we gave them shelter in a cave
so they could hear us praying in the night
and know if smoke curled from the roof
meant harvest food prepared at home.

When they moved off to the far mountain,
we still could see their fires upon the peak
to mark the daily rhythms of our lives.
By reference to their constancy of form,
our hopes were lifted to their heights.

When they changed residence to Heaven
our knowledge of loneliness began.
They lived too far away to bind a wound,
to bathe a fever, hunt for a lost mare,
pursue our enemies or prime the well.

These numerous god-beings fused
into one empty, enigmatic span,
now threatening, now seeming to protect,
but treating all villages the same.

Now going forth to seek the gods,
a skittish breeze, a vapor, or a shower
may be all that we can hope to find,
or bluer days an envelope of sun
that reassures our bodies for the day.

Since this is all the gods can offer now,
a stranger is the same as one of us.
It matters little from what hearth or town
this one has ventured forth to pray.

Now we are much too small for God to see
and God in Heaven much too big for us.
Our gains and losses have become our own,
And God has left us in our world alone.

[1967]

Out of Context

Petal torn from flower,
petal won't close or open.
Feather down from wing,
feather can never fly.
Fish glimmering on dry sand,
fish no more will glide.
Word apart from song,
word does no longer mean.
Star taken from the sky
shines not because it's stone.
Nor will I open, glide, or fly,
nor will I shine or signify,
for I am all alone.

[1978]

For Those About to Die Young

At the far-off rim
of the lonely verge,
let the shoring crumble
and like faulted cliff
slip down to darkling sea.

The fault not yours or God's
but witless demiurge
who fashioned you to be
(by such a spendthrift plan)
of non-enduring stuff.

Souls aweigh. On such a night
no harbor is enough,
when all that sounds is sea
and from the mainland of the self
comes the only light.

[1980]

In Solitary

This cage between the ears
is guarding precious stuff.
It is a fortress that may last
longer than the substance
it is made of. It wards off evil,
offers inner space, a room
to sit in on the polished floor
and chew the slender reed of reason,
distilling from its juice
the wine of thought,
the elixir of power
to wrest from the universe
that which is our own.

The foe is in the dream
that by stealth would enter
from the realm of chaos
seen through clouded prism,
with tangled wire protecting
a refuse heap of word:
the empty shells of sound
we fled from on the field,
the possessions claiming us,
the lie of begrudged moments,
friendship's lost occasions,
senility of heart.

These foes the while we sleep
may draw the battle lines
around our dreaming heads,
ask fealty of spirit
in an enterprise too foreign,
toss as a bare bone the soul
to the raging beast of war
that apes but is not itself
a beast that stalks the night.

But our citadel is sure,
a still and shadowed place
to tend the bloom of reason
where it waits upon the shelf.

[1980]

Ferrocarril del Pacifico

Breath of mildew turned to dust,
long shadows of the afternoon
squared into a black mirror
of interior imperfection.

Sat down and put my feet up
on the euphemism, "chair,"
reading by a 40-watt
until the groaning sounds
and the sidelong sways
built to a lurching frenzy
and it was time to hit the trail

Four cars to the diner—
Rio San Lorenzo, 96,
Finlandia, Kenya, 84, 88,
Rio Quelite, 252—
every ratcheted connection
a fresh scream of metal
and a blast of real live air
on this platform of adventure,
in this moving fun house.

Caroming in between
in a state of spastic grace
through the muffled corridors
with now and then a curve,
and lunging almost into

the tiny chamber theaters of
wagonlit repose:
spouses, offspring, layered
in a single berth,
fat mamas up in curlers
without corsets.
Four cars to the diner
and vary open seating.
More of waiters than of eaters,
more of menus than of food,
none of wine and none of brandy,
none of beer except Tecate,
nothing ala carte.

Number three with good, gray soup,
omelet brown around the edges
as the shredded lettuce.
Cold mashed potatoes
from an ice-cream scoop,
and one battered quarter-lime.
Three slices of Pan Bimbo without butter
Adios, 500 pesos, but no matter,
Devaluation's coming just in time.

[1982]

Ode to Benjamin on His Fourteenth Day

O he came here by the high road
away from any thing
that might have done him ill,
safer than a king.

His beginning was the word
and the word was light.
Now the sun has found him out
and he has no hiding place.

Now he surely knows
and never will not know
how light feels on his eyelids
and warmth upon his face.

Now he's swimming in the light,
arms and legs afling,
toward day-by-day forgetting
of the darkling place
and his special night.

Now he starts awake
and searches the bright room
with all his tiny might,
with veiled and curious gaze.

Now at last he finds
those pairs of eyes ablaze
with reasons why he came,
and hears the loving voices
that are teaching him his name.

[1984]

Lady Swimmer

to Eileen

Five-fifty in the morning,
the air is white and chill,
the water, a shade warmer,
is blue and clean and still.

You bend with grace and quietude.
You enter with due care,
alert and calm and serious,
no cap for your white hair,
as you offer up your being
in the watery lists of prayer.
Buoyed by gentle current,
your mobility is poise;
head lowered, scarcely splashing,
measured pace and little noise.
By turns the rhythmic arc
of each arm points up to heaven.
The parted waters soon rejoin,
your altarplace to mark.

In heart and head you carry
your husband, paralyzed,
four grown children and their issue
of whom God must be advised.
Ten laps each, for two of sons,
for two of daughters, ten as well.
Forty round trips in the pool,

enough to itemize their needs,
Dear Lord, may all be well.

Your spouse is almost motionless,
and even losing speech.
What can you do for him
but pray with all your heart
that his loving eyes and ready smile
may stay within your seeing?
For him you will swim twenty laps
and pray with every stroke
for deeper understanding
and strength and faith to stoke
the flames of rage and sorrow
that threaten your whole being

Woman in peaceful water,
leaning, leaning on its breast,
through your counting and your praying,
find the sanctity of rest.

[1994]

Ode to the Artist

Three Soliloquies: The Poet in Love

I.
You sit in silence,
look, as longing burns behind your eyes,
listen, as all strains of music merge
in one big overture to wished-for moment.
You walk, and hunting for the shining coin,
can scarcely lift your eyes above the ground,
your face a mask of unsmiled smiles,
and in your throat a well of uncried cries.
You cannot strike the metal to mint words,
and lacking filigree to mount the jewel
you would bestow, you sit in silence.
O contradictory mute, be not the fool
who ways of love thus carelessly decries.

II.
This hand outreaching and inviting,
with gracious palm and molded strength,
has scarcely touched, and at too gallant length,
the tremble of desire. Patience, wait,
the loving voice will sing your dreams
ever so gently. Before you is a music
of such span that living may not find its close.
Though senses cannot yet absorb, the spirit knows,
throbs with dumb wonder as the golden sound
envelops you in promise of your fate.
O poet-lover, hold your tiny peace
until your sheer captivity brings release.

III.
In melancholy mist
O poet, must you spend your days alone,
the object of your love to contemplate?
Is presence of the lover's knobby knees,
or itches, yawns, forgetfulness, or rage,
not fit to dwell within the golden cage
where beating wings identify the bird of love?
How can the ardor of love songs increase
where sounds pedestrian ever violate
the lyric moment? Would this love have grown
in supermarket, kitchen, or in bed?
or is it simply music in the head?
Accept it poet, just the way it seems,
for dreams are made of life, not life of dreams.

[1978]

Danger: Poet at Work

Do not reason with the poet
the wind of whose words
lures your thoughts away,
the rhythm of whose dance
makes you march out of step.

Incantations of the poet
may tangle you in dreams
that suffocate your world,
leaving you evermore
out of breath.

Seek the poet after hours
when speakers in two worlds
of words, diversely clothed,
may show carcasses alike
and similarity of souls.

[1981]

Leading Citizen's Elegy for a Poet

To begin with, you were poor
and picked the living trash,
scooping wisdom's crumbs
and draining daily dregs
just like other bums.

Nor did you grow rich.
The menu of delights
was generally forbidden
and unused joy became your lot.
Most splendid sounds and sights
stayed forever hidden
and you knew them not.

You grew up poor and free
as the world's non-paying guest,
dancing in dark corners
ticket-takers could not see
and sleeping in clean beds
prepared by those of us
who for some reason toiled
that the likes of you might rest.

You cracked between your teeth
seeds of passion and of wars,
or draped yourself about
in golden, finespun rags
that once had clothed the king,

or savored on old cups
the sweet and aging mouths
of princely whores.

From poor you grew to bold.
Fearlessly you swallowed
leavings of great feasts,
rich morsels steeped in echoes
of seduction and violins.
And when the revel stopped
you rolled beneath your tongue
the tiny jewels of poison
meant to keep the lordly loves
from growing old.

On a certain day in this great city,
brushing spirits with your kind,
you joined the mourners' walk
to the sacred burying ground
to shed a tear for Everyman.
And there at last you found
a place to rest that's free
of entrance fee or pity.

[1978]

Wintersing

to Kirsten Flagstadj

When all good listeners lie abed
in musky sleep, from sun to pole,
comes frost-flower she, afresh to sweep
nocturnal mist from huddled soul
and tune the ear to vision threaded
on her shining loom of song,
a snaring net of silver flung
from cloud-roof where the angels sun,
while she, sans souci, flies above
the peaks of ice whose tips catch fire
just from the shadow of her wings.

Then gliding down or letting go
she falls, a blossom in the snow,
petal-side up; and still she sings
the many sounds of love.

[1978]

The Song

for Edward

It is begun
of narrow note,
crescendoing
as bells are rung.
It tops the waves
and buoyantly its sails
are filled with sun.
And finally
it heads for home all quietly
into the harbor night.

[1979]

Christmas 1976

for Frank

As you are artist,
the love you cannot bear within you
pours through your fingers
to the brush and writes a message
that not all can learn to read.

As you are father, mate, and friend,
these powers dislodge
from the summit of your strength
and tumble down the mountain
so that none may pass,

As you are son,
you fan the embers on our primeval hearth,
and with sparks flying
you bank the fires of home.

Composer's Rule for a Good Poem
for E. G.

The poem should not make noise
but dole out words with care, and space between.
It should not actually be heard, but seen.
It should not thunder, howl like wind, or wail
or cast away to passion all its poise.
Whatever happens, this poem must not fail
to mean what it is meant to mean.

The poem should not be pushy or upstage
but rest upon its page or on the shelf,
remembering scarcely to assert itself.
Well may it imitate the brain of birds
(long known for minuscule simplicity),
avoiding all but one-syllabled words.

The poem waits quietly for a master
to set the pace and call the tune,
and will not arrogantly go faster
for fear of getting over with too soon.

The poem takes small steps, does nothing wrong,
moves with downcast eyes and sober mien,
toward the altar for its crown of song,
and then this poem will be queen.

[1979]

Who Cannot Ignore a Poet?

to E.C.G. who never did

Poets are too serious.
They never learn to play,
unlike most artists, who have
games to last a life.
Why just commotion of the colors
escaping from the brush
brings the crowd around to look.
But words lie mutely in a book
or skim the back streets on the wind.

And musicians!
They pound or scrape or blow
and tremble strings into a cry
or bounce them back to laughter,
or dredge up silver from the mine
within the throat to form
an arc clear to the sky.
Or, dipping light
from the river of the harp,
make music fit for Heaven.

But who cannot ignore a poet
whose dappled intervals of shade or sun
pass over quickly on the road
we follow to oblivion.

[1979]

Thank-You Note

to E.C.G.

A night or so ago,
a battle-weary poet,
engaged with every line
in mortal combat,
anguished in avoidance
of the dear enemy, rhyme,
wearied of resisting
the opiate of meter,
dreaming among words in the desert,
felt a thirst and drank
from the small rain of spirit
within your seven-line song—
a draught of understanding,
distilled from all the truth
so rich with your art,
so generously shared.

Reinforced, renewed,
and lightly touched with victory,
back the poet went to battle
and found the enemy gone.

[1980]

To Night

Al Fresco

[Sleeping Outside]

Moon on a string,
stars dangling from short wires,
sky puppets in the wing
for the Greatest Show on Earth,
which, like Our Father, is in Heaven.

Dark hallowed be His skies,
as with diamonds in my eyes,
I lay me down to watch
His everlasting play,
and the curtains slowly lift,
and the world has blown away.

[1945]

Sleep Song

Down down in the deep eye of night
beside the talking trees,
worn spirit I will now release
to swim in moving light.
As leaf-topped branching fingers
turn moon to globe of stars,
turning also, I will slowly cease
to shoulder the diurnal weight.

Comes now sweet breeze to touch, to lighten
hard noon's residue of burn,
in murmuring dark with strokes of moonrise
upon the weary head. All high-tuned
strings of watchfulness now loosed,
all burdens cast upon the fates,
until transparent morning, from behind the hill,
cuts a path through dreaming forest,
opening windows on the world.

[1950]

Song for Solomon

Apples and wine are good for the night,
they are comforting and sweet,
they are Biblical.
Their humors cold and warm hold at bay
both passion and the brain,
and if I choose to sleep
before the break of day,
they will cancel out my dream.

[1961]

Night

We who in the desert dwell
swim in an ocean like the stars.
Dark sea of air, ethereal, thin,
with ghostfish phosphorescing in
its currents. Not against our will
stay in motion while the earth stays still.
Gleaming we plunge into the chill
of air, and breathing, drink our fill,
and dreaming, dive for star-jewels in the deep,
and barnacled, sink back to sleep.

[1967]

Nightwatch

Every evening
carrying a heart that weighs too much
for my frail bed
I walk,
the only sentry of my dreams
I pace
the slender parapet dividing me
from sleep.
I scan the edge
of my known universe.
For the enemy
who will not show his face,
I weep.

[1979]

Christmas Eve Lullaby

The winds of all the world
are muted for your sleep,
the light of all the world
is softened for your eyes.
On the dark side of the star
we listen for the wind,
look to distant hills,
listen for your heartbeat,
and for the halting step
of pilgrims brave with knowing
that you have vanquished sin.
That same star glowing
warms your tiny space,
brightens crooked ways,
and radiant shows forth
the meaning of our days.

[1981]

Sonnets

Sonnets 1939

I.

Soft evening. Why an oldtime shepherd's pipe
could never sound more sweetly in a glen
than this, this music from the longing wren
who hides where apple boughs are blossom-ripe
and sings to me. Where is his love tonight
And where mine? I, who cannot see one star
in the deep heaven, nor can watch from far
the crescent rising that grows yellow-bright.
The winged one will spend no time in tears
but sing to call her to his side, while I
can say no word, nor lift up to the sky
one song of hope because these spectre fears
are giant shadows cast upon a heart
that only weeps because we are apart.

II.

If I could reach across the lighted town,
above the cold and scornful towers of steel,
and reaching, touch your fingertips to feel
the needlepricks of longing there, then down
upon this great confusion I might frown
with lofty goddess brow and strength as real
as dreams are now. What mortal thing can steal
or pierce a love-cast armor? Oh the town
is still. Worlds high above the resting earth
a pale half-moon is poised. Yes I have raised
my eyes to scan the dark, and I have grazed
the black walls of the towers. There is no dearth
of moving shades abroad. But you?
The morning's birth will find no trail of stars your
steps have blazed.

III.

I too put fragrant blossoms in my hair,
unbound it to the swift and capturing breeze
and hearkened unto Spring, with prayer to tease
my fancy till my heart should cease to care.
The flowers were dead. I shook them from my hair
and gathered new from bending, laden trees.
Spring flowers are fresh in growing. These
were brown and crumpled in the cutting air.
Why should they live? High gods have scorned
    the prayer
of Love who weeps in silence at their knees.
I would lock Love's gate and with the keys
sit steel-eyed, watching, on the hillside there,
withered blossoms clinging in my hair,
and scorn the gods whose laughter fills the breeze.

IV.

Rose-hearts bleed red where lately two have walked.
Bells across the town are sweet and clear
but winter-threatened leaves are shattering, sere,
above the glen where Love and I last talked.
Here, paying homage to the one Love mocked,
a wind-song makes great wailing at the bier
where I lie dead but listening, with a spear
straight through my breast. One hand I lock
to hold a last thread of the ancient pattern.
All else is gone. My face grown centuries old,
my eyes stark open and their light grown cold.
My hair lies streaming wild. Love made a slattern
who bartered laughter that was bright and bold.
Now Death stands black across the path of gold.

Three Sonnets 1968

I. The Sleeper

The dream was of another time in spring
with flower of peach, slant-fingered by sun's gold,
awash with breezes from a fragrant land,
alive with bird sound, crystal as a tear,
day ever changing with the shadows' length
'til moon spilled over fold of ripening eve.
In dreaming I did run with sudden fear
into the cutting wind, the eye of storm.
And there was death--the ring of steel on ice,
the air split by a shrill and winter bell,
and silence rising from the frozen ground.
Thus, not looking back, I took my leave
to hide and drop the curtains of my heart
and sleep to dream until some other spring.

II. The Dreamer

Cry not, my heart, for inadequacy of words
exchangeable as lovers' medium,
nor yet the insufficiency of birds
to sing away the daylight's tedium,
nor grieve that there are only certain ways
that arms and lips and hands can interlock
or cheek to shoulder touch, or brow to breast,
as love in finding love finds also rest.
In silence, silver strands of dream do run.
Across them, drops of crystal vision glide
through time and distance, not empty as they seem,
transporting love to love. Cry not, my heart
in loneliness, but laugh in dreams instead,
and turn the stone of every day to bread.

III. Night and Morning Song

My love the night has come upon my heart,
descended at the moment you depart,
unsheathing from its dusky cloak and hood
the talons fierce and long of solitude,
and fixing as in stone the fear
of all the mysteries that threaten here.
Now morning, come, and bring your smiling peace,
your tender, opening touch on grateful eyes,
your light insouciant breeze that dries
the tears of night. Come morning, hasten, come
to flower, to ripen corn, to fill with sun
the shell of dreams. Awake! now rise now run!
Now stir the ashes of the smoldering night
and set the torches of our world alight.

The Book of Uncommon Prayer

In the Beginning

Lay hand on us, Oh Word,
Our quick lives translate
to Eternity. If you have answers,
speak them fast, for Now is slipping
underneath us each as
time bears down the channel
and carries us to sea.
Transfiguring our deeds, Oh Word,
Bind act to speech,
that our lived meanings
be not blown apart
with every wind.
For should our image be despoiled,
who but God has sinned?

Morning

Hail Sun
who burns the evil out.
Our blood runs freer, purer
in your heat.
Sin scurries under rocks,
its venom dried to dust
beneath your light.
The shadows jostle in retreat
before your victory,
and virgin day comes wearing blue
to meet your eye.

To Music

Sweet music, have mercy on all of us,
who, meeting, speak past one another,
while the winds of solitude
that leave us deaf
set our thoughts adrift
to keep company with our silence.

Only your sounds, O Music,
speak to us for each other
or go echoing between us
in our round of partings,
and brave us for the void;
pouring golden to the rim
our private cups of sorrow,
our common wells of joy.

Communion

Spirit of strong spirits,
come purplestain our lips
with Heaven's humid kiss
and drench our dusty throats
with all the wines of love.
Cause our tongues to meet
with yours in flooded mouth.
Embrace us beyond breath
within your vining arms.
Now lay upon us hands
whose tendril fingers burst with light
and promise to catch fire with Spring.

Closing

Now we lay us down to sleep,
most undistinguished forms of earth,
more empty than a hollow log,
more aimless than a tumbleweed,
more silent than last evening's wind.
Helpless as a dragonfly
without bright wing to catch the sun,
we need no help for where we go,
there is nothing to be done.

Prayer for Peace

Help me to learn the lesson
from light falling on the land:
that intensity and clarity,
both properties of light,
are not the same.

Intensity pierces, penetrates, and pains;
is there before I know it,
but not in answer to a need.
Invading monochrome, it stuns to waken,
now damaging, now destroying
my safety net of dreams.

Intensity calls forth my drooping lids,
my darkened lens, my hardened heart;
oh then must I struggle
or it will have its way,
be finished all too soon;
and if seeing were believing,
it would leave me without faith.

Help me next to learn
that clarity is gentle,
glides through my lonely space
to be there when I waken,
cleans my corners of confusion,
sweeps my room of threat,
redefines reality, to trace for me
the boundaries between certainty and doubt

Help me to stay the course of intellect
in search of fresh perception,
to see at once, and for the first time,
both the mountain and the plain,
and the winding path between,

Help me to watch patiently
in this soft and easeful light
as the world unfolds more gradually
than I thought when first I bowed my head,
crouched low, and shut my eyes,
only to be blinded by a single, lusty ray
that pierced the membrane of my being,
eternalized my scream,
and made me claim all suffering as my own.

Lead me now to rest in this expanded vision
beneath the stroke of understanding
which, in undoing the furrows of my brow,
reminds me to accept at last
the role of being human.

Of Nature

Pine Tree

When winter's burdens press with chilling snow
and slender branches, captive to the storm,
from oak or elm down wind-washed bare streets blow,
and wet winds fiercer moan where winds are born,
then, piercing up and through the mist of morn,
we see your mighty slender-fingered spire
and hear your voice answer wind's in scorn,
see your crest, ice-laden, still aspire
to lose amid the crests of heaven its desire.

When winds of spring low like a Stygian herd,
and clouds are banked in blackness on the hill,
and lightning like a sweeping silver bird
makes far peaks for the moment visible,
then high you stand, a king unvanquished still,
above the broken arches of the wood.
Your spirit, winter-tested, stays to fill
the ice-bound vaults where lesser forests stood
and solace children of the spring with hope of good.

[1940]

In the Beginning

[A Desert Morning 1943]

This is the way Creation looked
the morning that it happened.
Fires still glowed in the forge behind the hill
and the edges of the earth were not smooth.

Crude color was streaked along the sky;
time enough later for pastels and the subtle blends.
Now bold blues and yellows, with
a handful of flame cast at the mountain peak.

This was the scent of the first wind—
peppery, inclined to travel with impudent speed,
unwarmed and sharp to the tender, curious nostrils
of the wild horse.

This saguaro was the first plant
and had no model of horticultural grace
so was overgrown and rough,
but tall enough to watch morning come over the hill
and strong enough for combat with the sun.

This may have been the first house—
square, unrounded of corner,
a brown-baked capstone to the sandy ridge of earth.
Small enough to evade the canyon's icy blast,
big enough to be seen by the first traveler
who came rejoicing over the land.

Snow in the Desert

The why of loving snow
in the desert in the spring
is not the shower of stars
on hardpacked earth,
nor the crystal on the cactus
nor the swansdown trim
on gourd or nettle,
nor the white draperies
the mountains crouch behind.
The why of loving snow
in the desert in the spring
is the ill-chosen time
and the unsuited place,
giving us a sign
that even cosmic laws
are made for breaking,
and not one bit more sacred
than any other thing.

[1965]

Rancho 6 a.m.

[Baja California]

Quelling, cool as water
still tasting of the night,
the new sweet air of morning
flows over sleeping fields.

Light follows the long fields
stretching beyond sight
toward the hidden ocean
that sends a healing breeze
to set small plants in motion.

Now moving through the fields
a man beneath a hat,
his back and path are straight,
his hoe across his shoulder.

He sings across the fields,
round notes, and without words.
Not cicadas rasping
or engine's pulsing drum
but his song finds the treetops
to wake a thousand birds.

[1974]

Dragons in the Wood

[Tzintzuntzan]

Believe it if you can
or grasp with me the scheme
of this quiet olive grove,
trees planted four centuries ago.

Trees scarred and rubbled,
thick and black, stand cancered
with bizarre, extruding mass,
or hollow as a staring skull,
each retaining semblance of a trunk,
offering branches to the sun,
leaning toward caress of rain.

Their truth seems that of living trees
that carry still the fluid of rebirth
toward one more spring, as witnessed by these leaves
with seeming magic green, and daring to
transform age through a much older power
by proving continuity of love;
thus they make not leaves only,
but, please note, as well the flower.

Time-stained and heavy with reality,
why do they keep on generating flowers
They have not fruited all these many years,
nor put one olive in one eager mouth
in payment for their place in the loamed earth,

but skirted mortality's fine line
with circumspection, playing as they should
the mythic role of dragons in the wood,
yet blossoming. For beauty's sake alone?
Or do they by provocating sign
give us new truth to make our own?

[1974]

Winterreise

Somber sweet winter,
I'm a stranger in your town.
No leaves throw shadows
on my dream beneath the tree.
Old wisdom cloaks desire
that no winter bird may see
how bare the turf that cushioned
tender, restless summer love,
as wind sings above my whispers
in the branches over me.

Winter, sad winter,
my flowers are white with frost,
dark roses of the sunset
grown purple and then lost.
The ice is thin where I would stand,
my steps are slower, soundless fall,
and nowhere, no not anywhere at all
are traces of my summer on the land.

Winter, my winter,
I'm stopping in your town.
Snow-wrapped in silver silence
dream the ages down.

[1980]

Sea Poems

I.

The sandpiper
trots on twigs
in a bird's body
with tiny rocking head
and interfering beak,
picking and feasting in the shallows
where the surf plays out,
leaving plunges to the gulls
and big mouthfuls to the pelicans.

II.

The tumbling whitecaps
and the arching surf
command our notice and our love
Look! we shout,
and run to play as children,
unthinking of the giant
who pounds and pounds beneath,
to be heard but never seen
through the splintered glass
of the crashing waves.

III.

Brooding seagull
banking to the wind,
hunts for his prize,
wheels over boats and trash,
over sand and smaller birds,

over playing children
and their parents watching.
Now above the waves
that hide the storehouse of his love,
where treasures gleam and dart,
the gull carves an arc of pure desire.

IV.
There were two streams—
one sea, one sand,
with moon and wind
enjoining them to meet,
wash over one another,
and make love.
But even as this happened
the same wind and moon
were pulling them apart.

[1981]

Sun and Puddles

to Gregorio, who taught me something about weather

Sun and puddles,
is the weather we like best.
It clears up all our muddles
and gives our minds some rest.
The breeze is oh, so soft, and fresh,
the leaves are shiny green.
In the pools along the sidewalk
our reflections can be seen.
The sky is smiling even though
we may not see a real rainbow.
New colors pop out everywhere,
and happiness is in the air.

[1992]

Thinking Back to Aulis
Songs for Iphegenia

[Written in 1982 as the basis of a libretto
for an opera to be titled *Clytemnestra.*
Composer Edward C. Garza received a
National Endowment for the Arts Grant in
1983 to work on the score for that opera.]

Thinking Back to Aulis

for Iphegenia

(chorus)
Sun has captured all the earth,
Noon is burning on the stones.
Together on the shore of time
are men whose goodness justifies their birth,
side by side with those whose sin
all life at once disowns.

Clytemnestra's First Song

We enter the valley of light.
Mules pound in the golden dust,
carts sway down the rugged slopes,
heavy with robes, with jewels,
with sweets for the wedding meal.

Quiet with joy and dread
I sway within one cart,
small Orestes asleep in my arms.

I hear laughter from the maidens,
their pretty heads, like birds,
turned toward one another
with the singing sound
of hero-naming on their lips,
each more glorious as spoken.

And of them all, Achilles
is the one, the peerless one,
my daughter is to wed.

(chorus)
What is Helen
but a face to hide the shame of kings?
as they make prayers to gods of their invention
and hymns to love they do not feel,
so they sing of Helen
and then launch ships,
carrying the wealth of cities
in bright armor, and the maps of death;
battering a daughter's dreams
for a nightmare of seduction,
spending virility and youth
in this wild and wastrel fashion
for a shadow of divinity.
No wonder the windgod's breath has failed
at this duplicity of passion
and that from the evil marriage
of men's lust and avarice
is born upon our earth
the beast of sacrifice.

Iphegenia's First Song

Where O where is the wind?
In back of the mountain

or lost in the wood?
Trees in your whispering
tell him which way to go,
out of the forest, over the mountain
down to the sea,
tell him to search the sands for me.

Come gentle wind
to this perilous shore
on the brink of my life
where I'm waiting for you,
If I must be a wife
I will marry the wind
and pair me with death no more,

(Chorus—of Agamemnon and Clytemnestra)

They met in a bare room,
a deathly universe
of four walls, and silence
giving back the sound
of that one question:
Will you kill?
Will you kill her?
Will you kill your child?

(—of Iphegenia running away)

Who pursues her? Who can it be
that frightened her away

from the rocky hill,
plunged her like a falling star
through the shady groves
down to the sparkling sea?
(—of Iphegenia calling for help)

As an arrow swift she flies,
arching neck like fleeting deer,
garments streaming to the dawn,
feet like waters of a brook,
running, tripping over stone.
She cries for help but is alone
as if no other were on earth.
She runs, but there is no escape,
and running, cries against her death,
cries as well against her birth.

(—of what is to come)

She is hunted like the deer
and like the deer will bleed
and burn in ritual flame.
But when the empty skies
are darkened with the cloud
that chokes the heart
and burns the weeping eyes,
even the blind will know
the meaning of this deed.

(chorus—the story unfolds in sin and suffering)

The pulse of love throbs wildly
in the hand upraised to kill.
What god could dare command this?
What man could dare fulfill?
It is he: Agamemnon.
The gods of war have bred
this father and this kin.
As a tree by lightning slashed,
his heart is split in two.
The father weeps, the king decides
what the man will do,
and in the very shadow
of the father's agony,
the king will cast her life away.
Iphegenia will be dead.

Iphegenia's Second Song

Father,
in simple syllables
of a trusting child
your mercy now I plead,
remembering how strong and tender
your embrace, your promises of bliss,
and on my infant cheek,
your loving father's kiss.
Now not joy but life I seek,
Foreswear then this deed!

Iphegenia's Third Song

Mother, it is time,
oh it is time,
the moment is at hand
to quit our tears and grief,
to lift our heads and stand
as rock-rooted hilltop trees,
bent, not broken, in the storm
yet stripped of every leaf.

Clytemnestra's Second Song

Agamemnon, hearken, King!
That red glow in the gulf of night
toward Troy—is it fire or blood?

Your thousand ships will soon be mooring
off the coast of victory
and still you do not know
what ransom you have paid
or what your crimes have bought.

On to your victory—it is close.
Savor conquest, taste it well;
for each ship, count one year of infamy.

A thousand years of burning shame
made hundredfold by all the sorcery
of a mother's grief—
a hundred thousand years of Hell!

Iphegenia's Fourth Song

I will put aside my life
as a bride leaves childish ways,
and keeping back my tears
will show the dignity
becoming to a wife.

Holding my head
I will move toward the dread altar,
seeking answers from the sky
when my step begins to falter.

Walking as the chosen one,
as the promised bride,
wedding for Eternity
with Death at my side.

(chorus—farewell to Iphegenia)

Sing to her long sleep,
sing to her last breath,
wrap her in veils of night,
cradle her in death.

Clytemnestra's Third Song

Child of my body and my heart,
my head says you are gone
but the light breeze of morning
is your hand upon my face,
and the small sound of birds
is your greeting to the day.

Sun glistening on the palm leaves
turns your hair golden also,
and the bees are circling
in the groves of afternoon
around a fragrance that is yours

You are here. It is I who am gone
from the center of my being.
I have gone to stand watch,
a sentinel among shadows,
and wait for your father. Yes,
child of my body and my heart,
I am waiting for the King.

COLOPHON

One Free Crystal Moment was designed and
typeset by Harrison Shaffer for Whitewing
Press. The text is Adobe Caslon Pro, based on
William Caslon's original typeface and drawn
by Carol Twombly in 1989. The display type is
based on Delphin, designed by Georg Trump
in the early 1950s and released by the Weber
type foundry in Germany.